Happiness 101

Igor Flikop

Scotchbrook Health Publications

Introduction

Over the years, I've been writing down what I felt, thought, and observed on living a happier, healthier, more successful life, and at the time I started working on this book, at the age of 33, I had several hundred pages of the inspirations and wisdom.

This little book is the collection of my favorite advice, ideas, and insights. I hope you like it and find in it something that can help you improve your life.

To my family and everybody who
wants to live a better life.

Enjoy simple things.

Spend time at a place where
you feel that you belong.

Do a good deed.

Give sincere compliments.

Change yourself, rather than trying to change others.

Do what you feel is right.

Have a healthy hobby.

Have a friend who accepts you
just the way you are.

Have a friend who is trusting and trusted.

Give yourself a pat on the back more often.

Reach out to somebody like you.

Stop putting yourself down; you're better than you realize.

Accept yourself!

A person trying to make you feel inferior is always wrong.

Remember that the bad guy could be a good person having a bad day.

A key to success is the right timing.

Take action when it feels right.

Try to stay calm during arguments.

Concentrate on the positive.

Be generous.

Do what makes you feel young.

Seek quality rather than quantity.

Work because you like the job rather than because the boss is watching.

Find an enjoyable way to stay fit.

Success often has roots in love.

Try motivating through rewards
rather than punishments.

Focus on your strengths, rather than weaknesses.

Once in a while, take a nap in afternoon.

Once in a while, spend some time alone.

Spend some time without business worries.

Spend some time just doing
nothing.

Pray for someone; root for
someone.

Help somebody.

It is a blessing to realize what's important in life while you're still young.

Don't let anybody talk you out of doing something you know is right.

Get comfortable.

Learn from your mistakes and others'.

Forgive yourself more often.

Try discussing the problem
openly and honestly.

In school or in life, be a good student.

Be a good sport.

Wear clothes in harmony with your personality.

Try to start off the important day on the right foot.

Stop forcing yourself and start doing what you really want to do.

Spend a day doing the things you like.

Learn from everyone you meet.

Learn how to bring out the best in yourself and others.

Experience people at their best.

Meet the people who've made it.

Try taking one thing at a time.

Let God be your best friend.

Be the one to tell the good news.

Focus on the positive in yourself
and others.

Eat fruits and vegetables.

There's nothing like living with a clear conscience.

Live your life so, that you'd be proud to share it later with your grandchildren.

Live your life so, that you'd feel comfortable talking about it on television.

Don't internalize bad emotions.

Talk about your problem with someone who has the same problem.

Focus on making the best things in life happen to you and your dear ones.

Thank, help, and reward the people who helped you.

When you have a problem, don't spend time worrying. Take action, do something to find a solution.

The cause of many problems is a misunderstanding.

Have a grateful heart.

Let love help you discover the best things in life.

Make the big decisions when you feel your best.

Compliment people in the presence of their loved ones.

Don't begin anything in anger.
Begin in love.

I've found that keys to success in a relationship are communication and trust.

When angry with a friend or loved one, wait till you're calm and talk to them about it.

If somebody mistreats you, remember they probably have done it because they have been mistreated by someone else.

Rather than motivating yourself by saying: "I *must*...", say: "It *would be better to*..."

The right attitude is half of success.

Discover a way to make yourself and the other person feel good instantly.

I've found that one of the most important things in a relationship is to be sincere.

Spend time doing something
that's both healthy and fun.

Cherish the places that feel like home.

Don't let blaming yourself
become a habit.

Have some fun every day.

Don't drive or live your life
looking back for long.

Remember that sometimes the quickest way to clear the air is tell the truth.

To help heal and cure bad feelings,
try writing them down.

Talk about your problems with someone you can trust.

Resist doing or saying a wrong
thing when you're angry.

Resist making a bad habit.
Break the ones you have.

Experience the people who want to make other people happy.

Live a day so that you'd feel
like you've lived a month.

I've found that one of the most important things in a relationship is to feel appreciated.

Don't waste time worrying about things that are far away and will probably never happen.

When you deal with people,
remember that no one likes
to be forced.

Almost everybody enjoys feeling important.

Don't be quick to take seriously
those who criticize you.

If you have one bad experience,
try to have two good ones
before the day is over.

Stop making each other feel guilty.

Stop spending time arguing about who is at fault. Concentrate on finding a solution.

Exercise when you are in the mood for it.

It's healthier to express your anger than to internalize it.

Remember your past successes.

Count your blessings.

If somebody mistreats you, don't be quick to get angry. They could be in trouble and need help.

Try to keep it fair and clean when you argue with your loved ones and friends.

Think of ways to make somebody's day.

Remember that sometimes you have to lose a little to win big.

Resolve the conflict and live without grudges.

Find the positive in bad
situations.

Learn it from the experts.

Learn important things that nobody else in the company knows. It will make your job more secure.

Discuss your work with someone who wants you to be successful. Talk about your health with somebody who wants you to be healthy.

Discover what it's like to live
without pushing yourself.

Focus on becoming what *you* want to be.

Slow down and make sure you're heading in the right direction.

Do what makes you feel good
about yourself.

Be able to do one thing better than anyone else can.

Begin a day by thinking: where to go and what to do, to make something good happen to you.

Have a hobby that keeps you young at heart.

If having problems in your relationship, remember the best cure could be forgiveness.

To help heal a relationship, try doing together something you both love.

If feeling down, try doing
something you like.

Watch a movie or read a book where someone is in the same situation as you are.

To get ideas on how to improve your life, try talking with someone else about improving their life.

A key to success is a good
self-image.

Don't discuss sensitive matters
when you or the other person
are angry.

We trust what we experience
rather than what we hear.

If you have a conflict with a friend or loved one, remember that this could be the opportunity to make your relationship better.

To help improve concentration,
try having in front of you something beautiful or something
you like.

If you're in a bad relationship, don't be quick to think it's because there's something wrong with you. The real reason is probably something else.

To help cure a loss of appetite,
try eating something you like
when you like.

Sometimes the quickest way to set yourself free is to forgive.

One of the best things you can do for your loved ones is be well.

Do what helps build self-esteem.

Spend time at a place where you feel comfortable and free to *just be yourself.*

Find an outlet for your anger.
(Not family or friends.)

Solutions to many big problems
are simple.

To help forget your troubles, try changing your surroundings.

If feeling down, try having
a positive experience.

If you have a problem in your relationship, try talking about it with somebody who wishes both of you well.

Follow your heart. It can be
the best trip of your life.

Do what you want to do.

Do the things you love.

Spend time with somebody
who wishes you well.

Be romantic.

Have a relaxing hobby.

A key to success is *liking what you do.*

You deserve to be treated well
almost all the time.

Find a place in life where you
fit in well.

To set yourself free from something, try getting involved in something else.

Sometimes the best cure for bad feelings is talking.

Live vicariously through your children and grandchildren.

Live vicariously through
your heroes.

Have more hobbies and fewer chores.

Give people what they *really* need.

Talk with someone who shares
your interests.

Give food to a homeless person.

Keep it simple.

Believe in love at first sight.

Do something nice for someone
you care about.

Enjoy your life!

Notes.